26 letters and 99 cents

BY TANA HOBAN

GREENWILLOW BOOKS, NEW YORK

This one is for Candace

Soft Touch letters and numbers used in this book are available at most toy stores or through International Playthings Inc., 116 Washington Street, Bloomfield, N.J. 07003

The photographs were reproduced from 35-mm slides and printed in full-color.

Printed in Hong Kong by South China Printing Co.
First Edition   24 23 22 21 20 19 18 17 16 15

Library of Congress Cataloging-in-Publication Data

Hoban, Tana.   26 letters and 99 cents.
Summary: Color photographs of letters, numbers, coins, and common objects introduce the alphabet, coinage, and the counting system.
1. English language—Alphabet—Juvenile literature.
2. Counting—Juvenile literature.   [1. Alphabet.
2. Counting.   3. Coins]   I. Title.
II. Title: Twenty-six letters and ninety-nine cents.
PE1155.H57   1987   [E]   86-11993
ISBN 0-688-06361-6   ISBN 0-688-06362-4 (lib. bdg.)

Aa

Bb

Ee

Ff

Gg

Hh

I i

J j

Kk

Ll

M m

N n

Qq

Rr

Ss

Tt

Uu

Vv

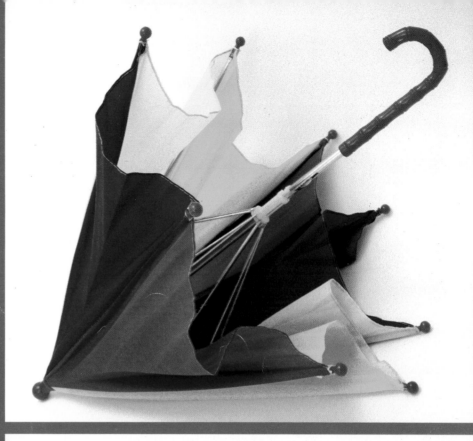

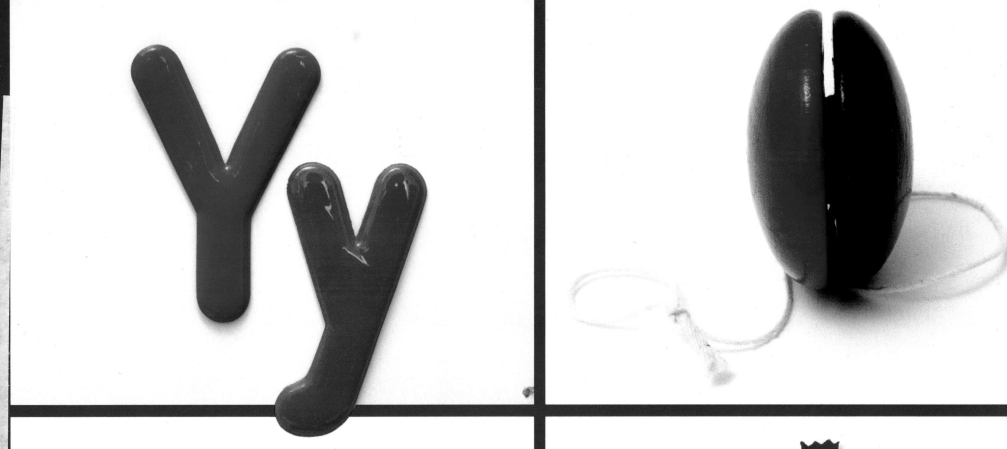

TURN THE BOOK AROUND FOR 99 cents

60

80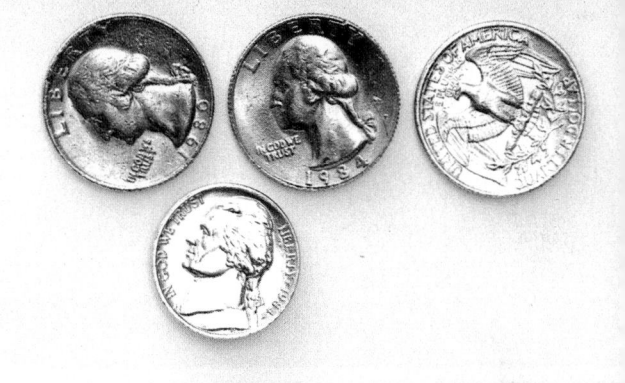

70

90

99

TURN THE BOOK AROUND FOR 26 letters

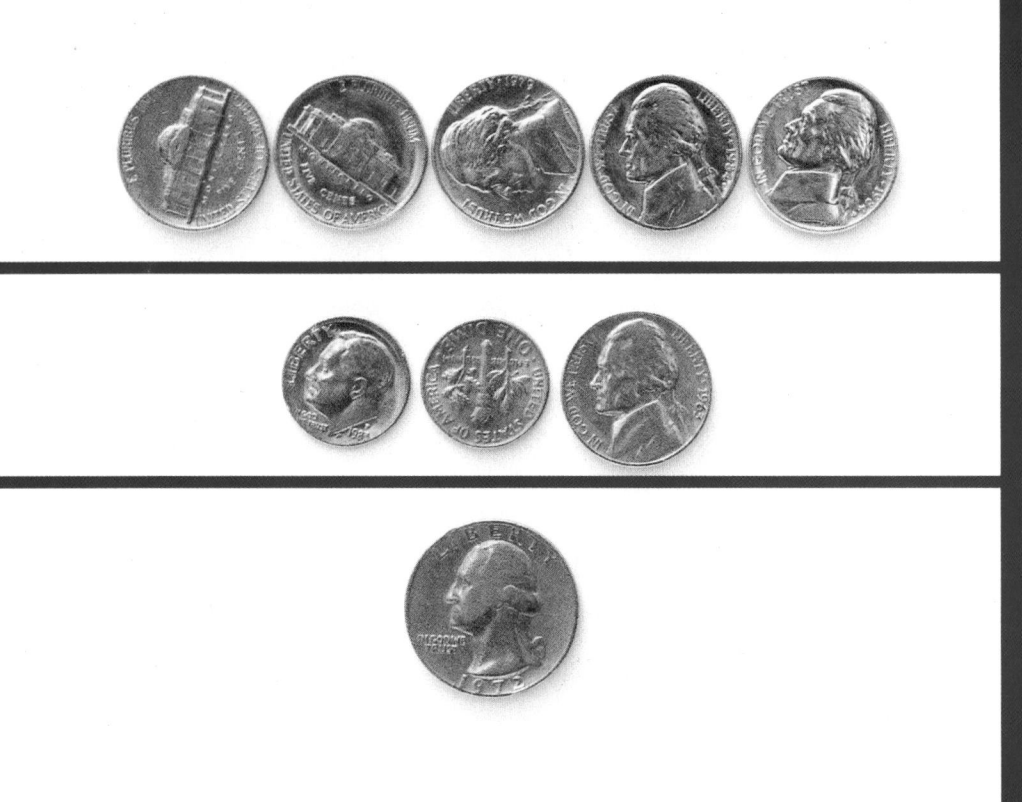

25

26

19

20

15

16

This one is for Candace

Soft Touch letters and numbers used in this book are available
at most toy stores or through International Playthings Inc.,
116 Washington Street, Bloomfield, N.J. 07003

The photographs were reproduced from 35-mm slides
and printed in full-color.

Printed in Hong Kong by South China Printing Co.
First Edition   24 23 22 21 20 19 18 17 16 15

Library of Congress Cataloging-in-Publication Data

Hoban, Tana.   26 letters and 99 cents.
Summary: Color photographs of letters, numbers,
coins, and common objects introduce the alphabet,
coinage, and the counting system.
1. English language—Alphabet—Juvenile literature.
2. Counting—Juvenile literature.   [1. Alphabet.
2. Counting.   3. Coins]   I. Title.
II. Title: Twenty-six letters and ninety-nine cents.
PE1155.H57   1987   [E]   86-11993
ISBN 0-688-06361-6   ISBN 0-688-06362-4 (lib. bdg.)

26 letters and 99 cents

BY TANA HOBAN

GREENWILLOW BOOKS, NEW YORK